Email Etiquette

I0005248

7 Easy Steps to Master Email Writing, Business
Etiquette, Email Productivity Hacks & Remote Teams

Lawrence Finnegan

More by Lawrence Finnegan

Discover all books from the Communication Skills Series by
Lawrence Finnegan at:

bit.ly/lawrence-finnegan

Book 1: Body Language

Book 2: Assertiveness

Book 3: Conversation Skills

Book 4: Persuasion

Book 5: Make People Laugh

Book 6: Small Talk

Book 7: Social Skills

Book 8: Email Etiquette

Themed book bundles available at discounted prices:

bit.ly/lawrence-finnegan

Copyright

Table of Contents

Introduction

Welcome to "Email Etiquette". For as long as people have been writing, people have been writing to each other. Some saw the advent of computers and word processing as the death of personal writing, but it took two computers to send each other messages. Suddenly, possession of a robust and clear writing voice became more critical than ever. When so many of us make decisions based on feelings and intuition, knowing how to express ourselves via email can be powerful. Not to worry, power players, most of this guide is aimed squarely at the professional and formal settings.

In the following chapters, we will discuss email etiquette and those places where the skills we develop here overflow into the rest of your life. Because what is email but the written word? How many of us have struggled to find just the right way to say something? Yes, when you sharpen your prose enough, you improve the way you construct sentences, which makes even your speaking voice improve.

You can spend the rest of your life sending out mediocre missives or spend a little bit of time improving your writing and letters in particular until you get to the point that you prefer sending important information through email. Develop a habit of regular newsletters and watch as your inbox begins filling up with friends and family instead of the usual spam, receipts, and promos.

While I may be *a tiny* bit biased, I believe that anyone can learn how to craft cunning, concise correspondences to create more cunning communication, and keep kin closer! Sorry, that's "alliteration," just one of many poetic devices you can use when you don't feel like using ALL CAPS to make a point.

Let's get started!

Chapter 1: Step 1 - Learn the Basics

The good news for many of us is that the traditions and formula of email are almost exactly like the pen and ink letter you might be used to. Snail mail's similarities to email means, young people, that most of the tips and foundational lessons I supply herein will carry over to handwritten correspondence, an art waning, which can be all the more impact for its scarcity. While we will learn which of the following lessons can be applied outside the cyber realm, our primary focus is on email and all its facets.

That said, it is E*mail*, and the roots back to written letters- even telegrams and other physical forms of expression- can teach us most of what we need to know to thrive in an electronic medium.

Similarity to Letters

Starting at its most basic, email follows the general form of written letters we learned in school: greeting, body, closing, and signature. Sharp readers will notice the lack of "heading" in that list, but the info which we used to put in the upper right-hand corner is now automatically entered on the email's time stamp or entered under your signature. There's CC (used to mean "carbon copy"), Subject, and a few others we'll outline further on, but most of the classic formula holds over.

Official correspondences still have a **letterhead** at the top, featuring a logo or symbol of the organization, usually centered, though the left corner is not uncommon. In the past, the right corner of the page contained the heading so it could also hold the logo
now.

The top is all by way of introductions, your business or organization's first impression. The reader can feel reassured seeing a physical address, phone number, and maybe another method of communication. So many fly-by-night internet companies exist (and then don't exist) that having established channels like phone and physical addresses as an option can give the recipient confidence.

Greeting
Dear Reader,

We use the word "dear" to mean beloved or at least precious, though it is boilerplate perfect as the greeting of an email. "Hi [name]" is also acceptable, though a good deal less formal. "Hello [name]," "good morning/afternoon/evening [name]," and "greetings [name]" are also good openings that are friendly, inviting, and work appropriately.

We can use the less warm greetings for any number of reasons. Usually, it's because the message is "cold," There has been no prior contact with the person. Cold is a perfect word when related to writing because using any of these openers on people you know or existing contacts would be "cold" in the emotional sense, too!

- Dear Sir/Madam
- To [name]
- To Whom it may concern
- I hope this email finds you well
- Allow me to introduce myself

Many of those sound familiar because they've been in use for centuries. In the case of a cold open, you might just want to put the point of your message in the greeting, as advertisers often do. Dear allergy sufferer, dear job seeker, and dear thrifty shopper are all greetings that quickly tell you exactly why your attention is desired.

Make sure your greetings are pointed at the target as precisely as possible. Why be cold when you can warm them up? After all, the first thing they read is the hook, and unless you sink it deep, you won't be able to reel them through the rest of the message. Only sales teams worry about reeling in fish, though, so consider this a stretched metaphor on making sure you entice, warm up, or otherwise welcome the reader.

Body

Here is the bulk of your message. Business emails must be quick and to the point; answering or asking need to know information only.

Personal emails should be as long as they need to be to carry your feelings as well as the needful stuff, too. As we'll see further on, this is where the magic happens- even if that magic is just the everyday wonder that is human thought translated to symbols and then decoded by another. Undoubtedly, our ability to take information from our brain and encode it into a form another person can understand was one of the crucial components of turning a flourishing village into a civilization.

Grandiose? Maybe, but you cannot deny the power of the written word, and like any skill, it can be taught, developed, and improved. Do not let people use terms like "natural born" or "inherent" unchallenged when talking about traits that come from hard work and practice. If you want to be an influential writer, write. Persuasion and relationship building so often focuses on interpersonal communication we almost forget that the physically separated had written letters for centuries.

Closing

Just like the greeting, the closing should match the tone you want to set: friendly, casual, professional, cold, or whatever. Having written this much, you should have a pretty good idea of the type of send-off to include.

Warm

- Best regards
- Sincerely
- Best wishes
- Love
- Many thanks

You may also restate your call-to-action in the closing if you wish to end with your topic still "ringing in their ears."

Extolling

- I look forward to hearing from you
- Speak to you soon
- Let me know what you think

Be careful of overplaying your hand or coming across as pushy because adding urgency to the closer is as direct as you can get.

Signature

Simply put, this is where you state who sent the message. While software exists to let you insert a digital signature, that is a bad idea for information hygiene reasons. You should only use your signature to seal a legal document, so throwing it into every message you send can be dangerous. Beyond you or your organization's name, on professional emails, be sure you include additional contact info. Contact info and the date are placed in the header in a physical letter.

It includes as many alternative communication channels as you care to have.

PS, Postscripts Are Obsolete

I have also seen people insert quotes, slogans, and final solicitations here, making the signature a sort of default PostScript. Seeing as how PS is usually considered an old-fashioned, even unprofessional element to add, using the signature space for that function is not a bad idea. However, you must realize that postscripts have fallen out of favor because you should just add any content you *need* to include to the body of the email. Postscripts only existed because you couldn't go back in and add information once the ink was down.

Professional correspondence should not use a PS. Postscripts should be reserved for casual or friendly emails if you use one at all. If it is important enough to include in the message, it's important enough to insert into the body. Since it goes below the signature, some people will not even see it, being cut off by the bottom of the screen or not scrolling down far enough- because no one looks for messages down there anymore; a bit like after-credit scenes in movies before the Marvel age. If you feel so inclined, be sure any PS content is off-topic, trivial, or otherwise not "need to know."

Differences

The electronic medium has created changes for the better. The ability to edit, add media, and include more than one person is a revolution in our ability to communicate remotely.

Headless

Computers add a timestamp automatically, and what *was* included in the header, additional contact info, is now included in the signature. While eventually you will have to delete your inbox, anyone can mark a message to archive. Also, you have to consider accidental or intentional over-sharing, but you also have to remember that a digital message can be forever for all intents and purposes. You have to wait a long time or go to extreme lengths to delete information from a hard drive totally.

Subject

Email showcases the subject line, and its high visibility makes it your chance to draw the reader's attention. Succinct, powerful, and otherwise potent, the subject of an email should make it clear what the body is about. Wax poetic, get punchy, and otherwise plan to penetrate the reader's routine. At this point, we all have email, so we know the drill: the subject is visible after the sender and precedes the amount of the body your screen size allows.

Poetry-- we finally have a business application for all those English majors who favored packing as much emotional punch into as few words as possible!

Your subject line is the thesis, most of the point of the email. Sometimes I will go back and edit the subject line after I've completed the body because, through writing, I've clarified *to myself* what I am saying. Getting a thought out of your brain and into a concrete form forces you to think about it in a different way than if you had never expressed it, such as the power of journaling, diaries, and logs, as well.

CC

Infinite perfect reproductions forever and, if saved, a virtually endless archive. CC means carbon copy, and the dreaded "replay all" has mercifully been depreciated from most interfaces. The endless copies part tripped up so many early users, with accidental Replay All and intentional sharing of private messages still an issue. While we go over the dangers and solutions to emotional writing next, remember that you are potentially writing for an audience: even with secure encryption end to end, a user can still be hacked or feel generous with your messages.

Chapter 2: Step 2 - Never Send Angry

Even more true for the electronic mediums such as paper and ink, you cannot afford to go off half-cocked in the modern age. People used to write angry but had time to cool off as they got out an envelope, stamp, addressed it, and made their way to the mailbox. No such cooling period is present with an email. If your words-per-minute matches your train of thought, it might be possible to fire off an email without even having thought about it!

Passion and Purpose

So you've decided you're so angry, you're going to write a letter. Even if you do not send the thing, the process of writing out your feelings can very often improve your perspective on them. You may revise, rephrase or even think about sending the message altogether. It would be best to reread and modify anything you write in any case, and that goes double for messages with a targeted audience.

You should never squander the ability to perfect your messaging. All too often, we fall into the habit of hammering out replies but don't give ourselves the benefit of a revision. When an email is going to a crucial recipient or contains important information, give yourself the time to reread the body of your message and try to put yourself into the shoes of the target. When a message is truly significant, you may want to test it on a colleague or friend, or even random anonymous people online, to give it as wide of a test market as possible. Extreme, sure, but it's the same precaution we give new software, media, and speeches, so don't be shy about applying that level of scrutiny to essential emails.

It should usually suffice to reread it yourself, then make sure you reread the new content to be error-free.

Processing or Plotting

OK, so you've got a full head of steam, and you're crafting a carefully worded, professional, polite email owning your feelings, or leaving them out altogether, and expressing your position. You state your grievance and why you believe it is wrong, but now what? In a professional setting and part of best practices in your private life is to **suggest solutions and not just point out problems**. It could be that the situation is dire enough to make pointing out the conflict and eventual build-up-and-explosion crucial. However, complaints ring hollow and sound like childish whining without an action plan in place.

It may be that you are **processing**, and while there is no solution to the problem at hand you're putting your thoughts on paper (or screen) is a great way to work out complexities and interactions that may have gone unnoticed. You may arrive at an insight or form a more coherent understanding through writing; never be afraid, in anything you write, to take the last sentence you write and copy+paste it to the beginning if it comes together at the end.

Cooling Off Period

I know that Gmail has an "unsend" button you can use to recall an email you've fired off but only within one minute; it's a cheat, really: the message is not actually sent until the interval goes by. Once you get into the mode of professional, concise emails, the only reason you might use this function is to catch spelling and syntax errors. It is not something to rely on, and not every email provider gives your emails that sixty-second delay.

Take A Moment

Just get into the habit of checking yourself, emotionally and intellectually, before sending out a message. In a professional environment, this is part of the job description, and if the news is going to more than one person, you had better check it, double and triple-check, too.

You can trick yourself into creating another cooling-off buffer by getting into the habit of editing. *Always* **reread before you send**, yes, for editing, but in the case of a hothead, it will give you a chance to cool off.

20

The more significant the information, the longer you should polish it. The more inflammatory or emotionally charged an email is, the longer you should ponder whether or not you want to send it at all. Do not talk yourself out of communicating important stuff because it's hard to get out. In fact, I have found serious and complex issues are often easier to discuss and explore remotely.

A Safe Distance

Writing something out often gives us the time to process and cool off or perfect our message. Take advantage of the tools available: spell check, use a thesaurus, and web search solutions if you are stuck. As much as our life experience is unique, the situations themselves are often common enough to have information available online. Usually, it's a matter of learning what you *don't* want to do more than looking for what you will do. While your search may turn up someone in your exact situation, if you take a step back destruction the conflict, often you will find the forces at play similar to other cases.

Write it out. Get it down. If it turns into a personal odyssey, *great*, "you've taken your first step into a larger world." Obi-wan quotes aside, even if you don't take the writing process any further than professional, taking the time to parse your emotions from your thoughts and explore ideas from an external, objective point of view will only ever improve your product.

If you want to take your emails to the next level, there's nothing for it but to **do it.**

Boundaries and Balance

Do not let a potential adverse reaction stop you from sending an important email. Nobody will respect your boundaries unless you set them early and maintain them often. A day or two is pushing it- you *should* be upfront and tell someone as soon as they transgress, but that's another guide! When the moment is passed, but the issue still galls you, express it! Don't bottle it, don't wait for it to happen again. If you have established email as a mode of communication you favor, use it. On the other hand, if you have never emailed this person, a sudden email will carry *a lot* of weight.

State your intent. Do not beat around the bush and say exactly what and why you are upset.

This is the part where you reread what you wrote and realize you are being dramatic, decide not to send, and delete it. If you are correct in realizing this is no big deal, fine- you have saved yourself some social clout. BUT- you may be right. Maybe this person did transgress and is either ignorant of the error or thinks it doesn't matter. Knowing when to express a feeling and when it doesn't matter is a complex tangle of drives and aversions only you will be able to answer for yourself.

Suppose the email is a professional or customer service issue. The question is if you feel like dealing with it more than it's worth expressing or confronting. When we have a clearly defined ethos, whether religious, philosophical, or otherwise, it is similar to a business policy: we know precisely what a sin, incorrect action, or trespass is and have usually been given a prescription for making amends. However, outside of spiritual dogma, it is evident to most of us what unacceptable behaviors and demand a response.

Clout As Currency

The idea of the Favor Bank is simply addressing the instinctual reciprocity we all demand. You can make social animals in behavioral research freak out by rewarding one more than another for the same work- our drive for fairness is almost as deep as fear of predators and about as profound as language. Laws and customs around communication and behavior usually serve to underscore these kinds of instinctual urges, and someone whose demands fall outside of this perceived (or legislated) norm is in danger of overplaying their hand.

Greedy, needy, or drama queen-y/king-y are all anathema to communication; anathema (when not referring to a disease) means disruptive, detested, and shunned. When we demand an apology, go back and forth to get our way, or otherwise assert ourselves over others, it carries a psychological weight. Too much, and others will resent the burden; making a lot of concessions to someone is exhausting, so be aware of how much you ask of others. This is a profound lesson, meaning it penetrates every facet of interpersonal communication: balance your give and take; do not be a doormat or a constant taker.

Chapter 3: Step 3 - Practice with Casual Emails First

So, you've decided to take up the pen, er, keyboard in a meaningful way. Learning to put your thoughts out on paper (I mean the screen) is a process like any other. Lucky for you, making email is so close to the writing of pen-and-paper letters the amount of information has been evolving for centuries. Monks in the Middle Ages invented emoji (though clerics did not call them "emoji" then) for the same reason we use them: indicate humor or otherwise insert the scribes' emotion into the paragraph. Then, as now, emojis were exclusively personal and seldom, if ever, turned up in official transcripts.

First, we start with casual emails to sharpen our delivery with friends, family, and loved ones. Our informal contacts will not only forgive our errors but, as long as we make it clear we are actively working on improving our written product, help us locate problems we are blind to. Dyslexia happens on a smaller scale to all of us: we can read, write and even reread the same error, but it won't be visible until it is pointed out to us or we do some of the hard edit tricks further on.

Establish Expectations and Keep Them

You want to maintain consistency, be it casual, professional, or otherwise, and if you are serious about electronic communication, then make sending emails a regular part of your life. People will come to expect it of you, and the practice will give your mail readability and even sparkle if you work on it. Establish your voice, be funny or insert wit; people are bored to tears sifting through email, so make sure you work on making sure your words pop off the page.

Emojis are OK in casual settings, but avoid them informal messages. Tone and inflection are lost, but humor is an essential social tool, so make sure it is evident by shining a light on it. In-text this reads like "joking aside," "in all seriousness," and "no, but seriously." Those are all great phrases you can stick after a joke to make sure the reader knows humor was intended. While you want to use it sparingly in professional settings, just like a public speech, you can use a joke as an ice-breaker or soften bad news.

If the person we are getting a message from is always a bit of a goof, then when we get a ridiculous email, it's not nearly as alarming as if the same message came from our painfully literal grandma. By the same token, you might be the funny one, and working on content via email is like delivering to the toughest crowd on the planet: without the non-verbal channel, most humor falls flat- if you can write something funny, it is a rare skill.

Emotion on the Page

Feel free to go over the top to engage. Establish your persona early and obviously, so people know what to expect of you. Just like television production, if you want to express a feeling, you have to over emote *just a little* for it to come across *at all*. This takes a little fine-tuning, as your voice as a writer may be quite pronounced right out of the gate. Avid readers, for instance, can usually dive into creative writing of any kind and find they already know the rules.

Letting your personality shine through is good for interpersonal communication as much as electronic: we forgive a good deal of odd behavior when it is part of our expectations. You should know by now what your voice as a writer is, whether formal, casual, expressive, or what. You may have never thought about it, but most of us fall somewhere in the middle, alternating between humor, formal, and casual as needed.

Personal Email

Before business moved online, almost all the emails you got would be from friends or family. After the advent of spambots and mass mailers, one's inbox is so full of work, junk mail, and phishing attempts it is a real treat when we get a message from someone we know.

- Family Newsletter- Why should the company get all the glory? Create a newsletter to keep people up to date on what is going on in your life; this is especially true if you have kids- we *love* to hear about your kids.

- Quarterly Update- Maybe you only have a page's worth of updates in three months; maybe you make it tri-annual or twice a year- your friends and family would love to hear from you and about you.

- Funny Forwards- Be sure to personalize them, add your aside or commentary; this used to be the bulk of all email- be sure you add your personal touch or at least mention why you sent.

- Just say "hi." You don't need a reason, regularity, or purpose besides just reaching out and touching base- be sure to include a few details or in-jokes, so the recipient doesn't think it's spam or a hack.

Initial emails should be lighthearted unless there's an emergency or sudden development. Once you have created a writing routine, you can add more and more severe and heavy topics. Observe the good-bad-good in terms of content because, just like a conversation, we can feel bogged down and even seek to avoid a regularly depressing encounter.

When that is the expected channel, relaying important information should only be done via email. If you just start sending need-to-know info to people via email when you have been using text or calls, the chances of the message getting missed are greater. Once you have established this as a preferred mode of communication, you can begin perfecting the content.

Understanding

Don't get so hung up on being technically correct to lose the reader. If a sentence feels too cumbersome after it is written, revise it, condense it if possible. Write for clarity, and if you are unsure how it sounds, **read what you write out loud** as a way to make sure something comes out clear. Another lesson that carries over to other facets of your life, hearing something out loud will give you perspective and renewed clarity if it has been in your head too long. Not only grammar and syntax but the ideas and concepts themselves resolve into a higher definition than when we leave them in our head.

Practice writing out of feelings, situations, and experiences. You've decided to write more, so write more. Like a visual artist whipping out a sketchbook to capture a sudden inspiration, don't be shy about pulling out a notebook or phone to get an idea down if something occurs to you. Once you begin looking at writer's block as a creative dilemma, your subconscious mind gets a hold of it, and then you never know when or where the solution will pop out.

Style, Tone, and Voice

The line between your unique voice as a writer and the rules of the English language is as squiggly and personal as the one between poetry and formal English. Beyond comedy or wit, your personality can still be visible under any kind of words, as long as you are aware of your word choice and impact.

Even a professional email can withstand a bit of poetic license if it helps deliver the message. A clever simile, apt metaphor, or appropriate quote can all achieve the same sort of frisson good humor can, so don't be afraid to go broad, deep, or symbolic when trying to get your point across.

Social Media

The modern age is the perfect place to develop and master your voice as a writer. The novel Ender's Game contains a side plot about his older sister the movie never even touches on. A family of super-geniuses, she becomes an essayist whose ideas rattle the foundations of society. Avoiding spoilers, her career is hilariously relevant today, as social media has given voice to the silent and increased the range of the already vocal. "Social Media Influencer" is one of those jobs which would only have ever sounded reasonable from a sci-fi author.

Businesses have a presence on the same platforms we use to keep up with loved ones. We old-timers remember when Facebook was all friends and family, the occasional organization the rare aberration. YouTube was commercial-free, but those ads created the revenue that pays the Influencer. People love to complain about those ads and the "creation" of the Influencer, but there's little difference in my mind between a radio pitchman and a social media influencer. When you listen to a podcast and hear the host start hawking a product, it's carrying on the same tradition of "soap operas" and other sponsored content.

Once you begin making a profit, or even living, of social media, you have leaped away from the casual, personal style of emails to the far more rules-bound realm of professional business correspondence.

Forever

I think the lesson has been driven home by now: we are in the third generation to have internet access. It should be as standard as "please & thank you" or "don't play in the street." You should never post anything to social media 1) you don't want to live forever or 2) go viral, which means become popular enough to give your fifteen seconds of fame. Do not post it if you do not want grandma, the boss, or friends to know something. There are ways around everything, even with security settings, private messages, and apps that auto-delete.

Some folks have two or more profiles, one stays vanilla, and the others represent an aspect of the person they do not wish to share with the general public. Quite frankly, given many people's narrow definition of normal and propensity for rage addiction, having at least two social media accounts makes sense. If you are in a provocative line of work and engage in social activities that might shock the uninformed or narrow-minded (IE are legal but could get you fired), there's no reason to jeopardize your future because someone decided they don't like the way you spend your free time

Chapter 4: Step 4 - Master Professional Correspondence

As much as we try to exude our personality into our writing when it's friendly and casual, when your nose is to the grindstone, and the chips are down, it's time to pare down and get serious.

If you represent a company, the default seems to be formal and self-aggrandizing. However, more and more, the informal dress and manner of the younger generation of CEOs are making even business correspondence capable of humor or at least wit. Again, you will know if the company you work for is the sort to keep official emails and even ad copy punchy and wry. In fact, if the organization is unorthodox in any way, it will most likely be in their mission statement or even graphic design master key.

Check with your supervisor whether or not there is a formal declaration of voice, and then make sure an ask permission before launching anything more than a colorful analogy.

Less Is More

It is almost always in your best interest to be as brief as possible in a professional or advertising environment. People wind up mass deleting entire pages of spam at a time, so positioning your subject line and even choosing an apt sender's name can be a huge benefit. Auto sorting makes even desirable messages appear in Spam or Promotion folders, so always make sure your sender name and subject line contain as much info as possible.

Nobody is going to want to slog through a long-winded dissertation on why your content should matter to the reader; even personal emails shouldn't drift too far into tangents and extraneous details. Unless it's a love letter or to someone who really cares about your every passing thought (parents, lovers, best friends), brevity is a virtue.

Stick to the **five W's**, who, what, where, when, and why. Practice condensing long sentences into short ones and expressing more with less. Almost poetic, the ability to write small but concise sentences is where writing practice, in general, can help. Crafting small pithy sentences is as much of a skill as anything else. Vocabulary can help, but make sure you're not using words over the comprehension of your audience. "Juxtaposition," for instance, is a great word that means the intersection of two things that contrast but few people will readily know that.

Editing Should Be Reductive

In the professional realm, the process of review and revision usually removes words or rephrases for brevity *and* clarity. Occasionally, more information is needed, though if you find the content of an email requiring more than a few sentences of elaboration, state the facts and why they are relevant, then insert a link to a simple, elementary break-down.

I find that if I cannot explain something in small, easy-to-understand words, I do not understand it well enough myself. If the information is important enough to include, it is important enough to understand. Do your homework, read up and research; a well-informed opinion is stronger not only because it's defensible, but you will be able to explain it better. You will only be able to articulate your position if you know its foundations. Large enough organizations have a "subject matter expert" of some kind, and if they do not, it is an excellent position to create for yourself. As ever, when adding responsibilities outside your job description, make sure you renegotiate your wages.

We Edit Because We Care

Get into the habit of **proofreading**, **revising**, and *rereading the revision.* Mistakes slip through because you rewrite or add something but do not go back and reedit- work on prioritizing grammar and spelling. Even poets adhere to the rules of the language, even if only to subvert them.

A carefully worded, well-thought-out email can come out of left field if you have never sent something like that before. An unusually well-crafted message can feel forced, canned, and otherwise fall on deaf ears because people will think it's copypaste from someone else! As long as it is all in our own words, even those shot-in-the-dark emails will hit home. The software Grammarly is great for catching small stuff, but remember it is simply an algorithm and not perfect. Not only is Grammarly just plain wrong sometimes, but it can also winnow away your unique style and leave your message sounding bland or dry. Most word processing programs have some kind of spelling and grammar correction stuff baked in any way, so make use of it.

Hard Edit

After you reread something too many times, mistakes can get lost between the screen and our brain; eye fatigue, brain tricks, and being tired can make reading something for the umpteenth time counter-productive. Do one or more of the following to trick your brain into reading something again for the first time.

- Change font and size (make sure it's a font you can read)
- Change the color of the font (contrasting background)
- Change background color (contrasting font)
- Print and read the hard copy (change rooms, exercise)
- Read in a new setting (travel there, log in remotely)
- Wait; change tasks, nap or sleep, exercise (give the mind something else to work on)
- "Publish;" post it someplace private and removable (see it as the client may)

Content is King

Beyond the Five W's, your professional messages should be *primarily* emotionless. Keep your feelings and most subjective opinions out of the content of the body. If you're in a position where your expertise is called for, fine, but in day-to-day interoffice messages, you want it as short and to the point as possible. There is room for creativity, even fun, but if those are things you require all the time, you should have a dedicated channel or two just to blow off steam. Longer format messages for work need just as much time and fine-tuning as an author's fiction: the wider the audience, the more you want to fine-tune your delivery.

Once you've sieved the emotional, you have to filter out the extraneous. Use specific, declarative statements: unless there *is* room for change, do not use indefinite words. While you don't want to sound dictatorial, you don't want to inject a false sense of hope; that sounds dire but thinking a situation is flexible when it is not can be extremely disheartening.

Word Choice

There is no need to "define your terms" when using the dictionary on words you are unsure of. If you are uncertain about a word, only ever used context clues, or overheard it used, look the word up. Leave poetic license for the personal and casual; stick to concrete usage professionally. There might be occasions when you have to go back and forth to clarify or elaborate, but as long as you have edited and made sure you are using words correctly, the burden of proof should be on the other side. While it can be tempting to use big words as much as possible, you have to remember your audience as well as what type of feeling you want to instill.

In the case of turning to a thesaurus or otherwise agonizing over the perfect word, be sure to remember that sometimes a single word can replace a sentence or even paragraph. Still, if no one knows the word, you are squandering your target's patience. If the word truly encapsulates the entire point of your message but is obtuse, you can use the definition of this term as the body of your email.

For example, suppose you need to encourage teamwork. In that case, you could give a detailed explanation of the word "synergy" and find a great example of individuals working together to create a result greater than the sum of its parts. Of course, the word *synergy* got trendy and then cliched in the business world, but that's only because it was something everyone wanted. When you start turning to the thesaurus, make sure you stick to the "ah-ha" or "oh yeah" discoveries, resolving a "tip of the tongue" moment, and when you find a common term you were not thinking of.

Mass Messaging

While there's more to learn further on, the subject of emailing groups is too intrinsic to pour into a single chapter. All the lessons (and more!) on brevity and professional detachment come up when we blast a message across many inboxes at once. You have to chop your sentences into short, succinct, Hemingwayesque versions of a typical sentence if you are going to get your point across. In the cases of ads and simple messages, you can forgo good grammar and punctuation altogether; if the message is as long as a subject line, put it in the subject line and repeat it in the body.

Sound, animation, and even a little interactivity are possible in modern electronic messaging. Large-scale sends may benefit from graphics or infographics if the content is dense. Desktop software almost always comes with some basic slideshow and image-makers, so learning how, or developing from novice to practiced, is an *excellent* office skill set to learn (pro tip: pick up Excel and blow minds). If you go the route of making a PowerPoint or similar, use pictures, graphics, and as many tools unique to the format as possible but only if they directly apply to the content. Do not just string together a series of text-only slides. Sitting through a bunch of bullet points we could just as easily have read is a waste of everyone's time.

Group Dynamics

Dynamics are processes or systems characterized by constant change, activity, or progress, and in a person denotes a positive attitude, energy, and new ideas. Without a positive dynamic, you're never going to get synergy gong. Lots of Ys in that last sentence, but the fact remains, and you can get the ball rolling by priming everyone's exceptions in meeting invites and memos. If a meeting agenda looks like it could possibly be achieved through email or otherwise remotely, do it.

The Information Age and pandemic have created and then made necessary a remote workforce. Face-to-face meetings tend to get called out of transition or feel it's the only way to generate a free exchange of ideas. While it takes practice, just like anything, you can get similar if not the same results online as you can in person. Even if your company is still hung up on brick-and-mortar and face-to-face, you can still utilize the tools of 21st-century communication, if not their universal application.

When a project will affect others in the org, use email to get feedback from those affected individuals as much as possible. It would be impossible, or at least tedious, to do such wool-gathering in person, but an email to the project head and CC to all those affected goes a long way. Even if you don't get a chance to honor everyone's wishes, it will be known you got input from them and be appreciated. The insight of the "boots on the ground" workers is also essential.

Management passing procedural changes down from on high with no feedback is the definition of Ivory Tower management; such uninformed decisions appear obviously out of touch at best and be counter-productive at worst.

The Newsletter

A powerful tool of business, a carefully crafted newsletter can drive sales, motivate action and even acquire new customers. It is such a potentially powerful tool many companies exist which will handle your regular or routine information pushes for you. Again, this is one of those topics which is heavy with content and options.

Following the same format as anything, a newsletter typically opens with an ice-breaker or lighthearted introduction, goes through the topic easily and quickly (bullet points, images, infographics), and wraps up with a call to action or otherwise affirms the message. Establish the regularity and tone, then stick to it. More than anything, you want it to be engaging and even exciting; put content inside a newsletter that people will want to see, not just need to see. This is one place in a professional environment you can insert some humor or levity if only to reengage the disenchanted.

Search for "newsletter templates" or examples if you are stuck, but chances are you know your organization enough to put something together that will attract the most readers.

Chapter 5: Step 5 - Learn Time Savers

The digital content of modern living is both a blessing and a bane for its users. Mainly a benefit, the perks, and positives of the Information Age outweigh the negative. We can waste time online easier than anywhere else, and if you ignore best practices, you will very soon find yourself hacked, or worse! No, by the time you are in a professional position where mass communication is a part of the job description, you should have picked up the dos and don'ts. While we cover some of the basic cybersecurity information further on, this chapter will be covering the dos.

With all the modern computing tools at your fingertips, it can seem overwhelming. Future shock never hits as hard as when we're online, but email and electronic communication can be learned and mastered just like anything.

Upkeep

As hard as it seems to keep on top of, keep your inbox empty. Not as important on your personal email account, once you become familiar and comfortable with archives, labels, and custom boxes, you will find keeping your inbox clean as good of motivation as anything. Many email providers have begun to impose data caps on email content, anyway, so deleting not only inbox junk but also messages from completed projects and other obsolete stuff is part of best practices. Be careful with deletions, but even if something does get accidentally cut, the Trash file exists for that very reason. You can even adjust the time a file stays in the trash before it auto empties, so if you find yourself a little trigger happy on the deletes, make sure you give your bin a deep bottom.

Set Aside Time Each Day

If inbox management isn't your sole job, make sure you dedicate a little bit of time each day to the task. Best practices dictate you make it the same time every day in order to not only gel it into your routine but create expectations from your regular recipients, too.

Fast Turnaround

Instead of setting reminders or otherwise waiting, reply to messages as soon as you can. Procrastination is avoidance, so get into the habit of tackling requests as more quickly they come in; more significant volume email addresses will have a natural queue, so use the timestamps and subject line to prioritize which messages responded to in what order. All messages are not created equal, so be sure to keep your good eye on the subject of inbound messages.

Remember, even though you want to keep a clean inbox, it doesn't mean you forget that digital storage is cheap and archives can contain whatever you like. If a message seems like it might be helpful later, save it. If someone sends you a message in error, forward it, then CC the sender, so they're not wasting your time.

Digital Tools

If you haven't already, **create different folders**. One should be blaze red, all caps, and otherwise, be Action Needed. If the timescale is short enough, as long as you maintain an empty inbox, there's no reason even to go that far- the irritation of having something in there will be a reminder enough.

Canned Replies

"Copypaste" is slang for the time-honored tradition of copying and pasting blocks of text from one place to another. For that matter, computer programmers refer to coders who just duplicate other's software as "script kiddies." Still, in both cases, the practice is so common as to only merit mentioning when overused. Usually a term of disrespect, just don't use copypaste in places where your genuine emotions are called for, and you can use all the recycled text you want. Keep a file of common phrases or even entire sentences you use. A mainstay of IT departments, most inboxes fill up with easy to solve, common problems; making some boilerplate responses will save you time and sanity. Everyone likes to be addressed personally, though, so add a personal touch before or after the duplicated text if time permits.

Make a Fill-In-The-Blanks style format so you can personalize it on the fly. Make the fillable sections without spaces between the characters so you can simply double click to highlight, and then any text entered overwrites the selected field. Most email providers have a Templates folder already there for you, or at least the ability to make one.

Auto-replies

When you know you will be out of touch, increasingly rare in this day and age, you should make sure to activate an Out of Office Reply, so people don't expect you to get back in a timely manner. These can often be customized to give specific messages to particular senders, so make sure you note priority contacts and have crucial people forwarded details instead of receiving a "Please Wait" type of message.

Attachments

I cannot emphasize enough- on the top ten list of email mistakes, after errors involving sender, CC, or recipient, accidentally attaching the wrong file is a close second. Double-check the file you attached is the one you intended to send. Once the file is attached to the email, you can usually right-click (or ctrl-click on an Apple) and select Open to do a last-minute review.

Saving over or deleting drafts and only maintaining one document per project also makes sure you are not sending a rough draft in error.

Unless your job benefits in any way from keeping drafts old, getting rid of the inferior ones is always best.

Set Rules and Filters

All of the office-oriented email providers will let you set up rules to take actions automatically based on sender and other variables. Color codes, custom folders, and varying priorities can all be set up to help you reserve mental bandwidth for more pressing matters.

Defer, Delegate and Delete

Use the forward button without reservation. If a message comes across your desk that is not part of your job description, do not waste time on it. If your job likes to push them above and beyond mentality, make sure they pay you accordingly. It is all fine and well to give more than expected, stretch yourself beyond your role when asked to, but if the company is paying you at the bottom of your job's average pay, do not allow yourself to be used. The larger the corporation, the more hands are on deck, and the more likely a request gets misfiled.

Small business growth and slave-to-shareholder mentality in publicly traded companies both will create environments where growth for the sake of growth is the norm, so be sure to watch for expanded responsibilities to crop up. Make yourself indispensable but never allow yourself to get exploited. If your workload increases out of pace with your compensation, speak up. If you find your team too small, no one to delegate to, or your otherwise asked to do the impossible, give two weeks' notice. Make sure it is not a bluff and have new work lined up before leaving.

Asynchronous Communication

Establish as soon as possible whether or not you intend to get back to messages within 24 hours or not. In the global marketplace, the default (unless otherwise stated) replies within twenty-four hours of being received; this allows for people on the other side of the planet to remain actively involved. Of course, pressing matters wait for no sun, and once business is being conducted more than a few time zones away, you are probably looking at day and night staffing, anyway. Even if you *can* reply within a short amount of time, it is usually a good idea not to promise that unless you have to. A medium-length turnaround assures accuracy and allows for a sudden rush not to disturb your flow too much.

Delays and Excuses

If a deadline is missed or an apology is otherwise called for, make apologies and offer solutions. I never provide excuses unless the reason is requested for precisely the same reason the old cliché insists: excuses are like butts; we all have one, and they all stink. Unprofessional, after a certain point, they are immature, too. "Sorry, I know it will be late, you will see the finished product no later than Tuesday" is fine for most cases. For the most part, we all know that life gets in the way sometimes, and unless you've made a habit of being late or shoddy workmanship, no one will demand to know why, as long as they know when.

Chapter 6: Step 6 - Use Rich Media

We have been talking exclusively so far about "**plain text format,**" the default used when composing a message. While lacking luster, a plain email is far less likely to be flagged as spam, is lighter weight (less data), and is supported universally- all but the most basic of phones can represent plain text. However, there are options beyond the send button, and advanced users have many tricks up their sleeve. The more features you add, the more likely another system will misread or fail the addition, so be sure you use sparingly and test fire anything you create. Sticking to plain text guarantees every single part of the message is received, and many users are easily put off by too many bells and whistles in their inbox.

HTML

Using the markup language the internet is written in to give your emails more impact *could* be a whole chapter to itself, but there are hundreds of reputable sites to aid you in this endeavor, from What You See Is What You Get software to tutorials on writing HTML from scratch. Not every inbox will support all types of content, though you should not see any problems by sticking to the basics and popular (see also: tried and true) templates. Inconsistent rendering of HTML across all browsers means you have to use it sparingly.

Unless you want to learn HTML (easy for people with an ironclad sense of syntax and grammar rules), most of us begin with templates. There are thousands to choose from, so be sure to use keywords to narrow it down: professional, humorous, etc. Look around in the options and add-ons that come with your email provider, and chances are good you'll find some HTML templates at least. You may wish to forgo HTML altogether and use rich text formatting instead. Of course, you can use both.

Hypertext

At the very least, links at the bottom of the email which allow the reader to subscribe, unsubscribe and help or FAQ pages are not hard to add. There are link-making buttons built into most programs that handle text these days, so you don't even have to go outside the inbox for this one. Usually, the symbol looks like two joined links, but since this particular icon is not standard, you might want to mouse over all the icons around a new, blank email until you find it.

There are bad bots out there constantly scanning the internet for email addresses to scan and spam, so make sure any email address you send folks to is secured and ready for tons of junk. Making a custom email address for your biz is best practices for many reasons, cyber-security just one of them.

Explore Your Windows

Hover your mouse over all the icons around your email screens (do this in any program you often use, for that matter), click things if you don't know the word or if there are no pop-ups. Images, signatures, and more are available from most screens. Some email providers have "confidential mode," which ban copy, forward, and download, then sets an expiration date so the message auto-deletes. Make yourself familiar with all the options- I recently discovered that last one. Modern email editing web pages offer almost as many benefits as light-weight word processing software, so explore and utilize.

Rich Text

The format changes you are most likely familiar with: **bold,** *italic,* underline, as well as left/right justification, bullet points, and embedded images are all possible with rich text. It was only through researching this guide I discovered the name of these features; they are so universal to the "compose new message" screens across all the email providers I've ever used I had taken them for granted. Embedding images can turn into attachments, and attachments can turn into hosted files depending on how the message is read on the other side. So be sure to test anything you add beyond attachments; even attachments can get broken in transit, so be sure to check once delivered.

Conversion

It can be beneficial to use HTML or rich text even when you know some recipients' browsers will break your add-ons. Most inboxes will automatically downgrade a message to either make room or out of paranoia. An HTML will downgrade to Rich Text, and Rich Text can downgrade to plain text.

Chapter 7: Step 7 - Be a Remote Team Player

We have mentioned that you can utilize the power of group dynamics online, so let's look at exactly how we do that. The ubiquity of smartphones and the use of work computers or access from libraries and other public places mean there's no reason not to utilize digital communication in as many aspects of your life as will benefit.

Whether it's the amazingly flexible creation and revision process, the ability to collaborate with anyone anywhere, or just the sheer number of options available, the potential for the digitally written word to strike wide and deep is profound.

Shared and Collaborative Files

The most significant benefit to the remote team is cloud-based, collaborative files. Be sure to investigate all the options available and always turn change tracking on if it's an option. That will highlight and flag any changes made and by whom, usually allowing a note or comment as to why. The document is usually "live," meaning any changes made are updated in real-time, so someone looking at the same page need only refresh their browser to see the editions. Setting permissions will confirm viewers, commentators, and editors, making sure too many cooks don't spoil the broth.

"Too many cooks spoil the broth" is a perfect metaphor here, as too many points of view can muddy an otherwise quick delivery. While the power of collaboration and a free exchange of ideas is excellent, just like so much in life, there is such thing as too much of a good thing. Accept input from too many or uninformed sources, and the advantage of hybrid ideas flips to a messy or confused lowest common denominator. Choose a lead, designate roles and maintain healthy boundaries by relegating extraneous persons to observer status if you include them at all.

Establish Norms and Standards

Just like you work on establishing your voice as a writer and consistent personal emailing, make sure you set expectations early and maintain uniformity as a remote worker. As in all things, stick to deadlines, adhere to work hours, and deliver fast turnarounds. Do not start a position at a frantic pace in order to "put the best foot forward," or you set the expectation that you'll be running at that energy level all the time.

Organize, Prioritize, and Diversity

Suppose you hate computers and have only just begun to learn email: fear not. All the software (software is any program written in a language a computer can read) and hardware (hardware is the solid stuff: the keyboard, the mouse, your screen, and the machine itself) used in professional and casual settings is user friendly. That means it has been made to be as intuitive and easy to use as possible. Young people: if you have avoided tech stuff just because, same: consumer-grade electronics are made to be picked up by a random person and used.

Use a unified software package as much as possible. If you're using Google Meet, then Apple's Facetime for another, and then Zoom later, you will get confused. Not only does your mental bandwidth gets taxed, but your hardware can get confusing, too. Speakers, mics, and cameras all have their own drivers, and switching between many different programs increases the likelihood you'll crash or have bad sound or image. Breathe deeply, consult the Simple IT Guide and know that even the most capable computer wiz started as a rank amateur.

Still, if you have a method to keep them all straight and you've piecemealed a hodge-podge system of freeware and open-source, it is possible to at least get started with remote work without a corporate account or money for a software license.

To say nothing of how slow a computer will run when there are tons of different processes using system resources, a single software package will also offer a unified user interface, making the learning curve more manageable.

Open-Source Options

While some proprietary software is locked behind paywalls and passwords, if the program is widespread enough, chances are there's a free version or even open-source compatible option. Microsoft Office has a few clones: Open Office and Office Libre being two of the most popular. They are free, updated regularly, and designed from the ground up to be compatible with the major Microsoft Office products. While not a perfect solution, free beats cheap when you're just starting, and after only a few paychecks, or access to the company network, you can sometimes pick up an "enterprise-level key" through the IT department.

While business will "demand" Microsoft Office, I have yet to create a document with Libre or Open Office that isn't acceptable. Make sure the file extensions are correct because both open-source options I've mentioned default to their own native format, though both let you Save As a .docx or PDF.

Prioritize

Your email management software has rules you can create and a way to set up reminders. Even your personal email addresses usually come with a calendar and reminder functions. Color coding, special folders, and alerts should all be used to keep yourself on track. Make sure to use the tools given and take the extra second to set up alarms and target dates. Not only a tool for timed email responses, once you get into the habit of using a cloud-based calendar, but you can also create one for extended family, the neighborhood, or a friends network, too!

Work/Life Balance

When you are part of a remote workforce, the tendency is for work to come trickling in at all hours. Establish as soon as you begin a remote position the work hours; if they intend for you to be able to respond to emergent situations at all hours, your pay had better reflect that.

Turn off Notifications

Is your job paying you to be available 24 hours a day/is constant availability part of your job description? Will the world grind to halt if you fail to reply to an email that comes in at midnight? If not, make sure your inbox isn't dinging you at all hours by turning the notifications off. Sleep aside, your free time should not be free of charge: defend your boundaries. At the same time, as ever, be mindful of midnight messaging yourself. If you have established an email routine or business hours, stick to them. Create some breathing room between your work and personal life by giving yourself the benefit of actual free time.

Work Space

Ideally, you have a room in your home dedicated to working; closets, seldom used bathrooms, and odd corners have all seen duty as home offices when space is limited. If not a special room, do what you can to create a different environment when you sit down to work. Background music works to make your mind switch gears, though it has to be light enough not to engage your mind. Ambient, classical, smooth rock, jazz, and nature sounds all work.

Announce that when you are in that space, it is work time, and you can't be disturbed. Interrupting a good flow state is a real problem, so if you share your home, establish early and often your need for isolation. It is work, and you and them both need to think of it as your work environment.

On the other hand, you *are* home, so if you are in need of a break, don't hold yourself in place. Doing a small piece of housework or short errand is often just the thing to let your mind switch gears long enough to come at a problem from a fresh perspective.

Information Hygiene

If you do not know the person, do not talk about details that might lead back to you. Obviously, your address and even town are easy to withhold, but it is best practice not to reveal too much more if you are using your real name. While interoffice messages usually leave a firm enough paper trail to deter security risks, you never want to give too much when talking about yourself to strangers.

Always log yourself out of workstations, and if it is possible to double-check something, double-check you are logged out of any public computers. Library, hotel, and friends all have systems we may use- make sure Sign Out is always your last step.

Do not forward false information. At work, passing along wrong information is gossip or worse, and in your personal life, it is rude to stir things up based on spurious, incorrect rumors. The Information Age has a double-edged sword, as we can find anything to rationalize everything just as quickly as we can prove a fact. It is not hard to know what to believe, at least not to someone who's written a paper with proper citations or spends even a minute looking up who wrote what.

You will have passwords and usernames, but if you write them down anywhere, you may as well just Sharpie the things across your wall.

Passwords and Security

Think of a Username you can use across all systems; it usually has to be unique, and in some cases, IT will select your username for you. Information Technology and Info Security people will tell you it is best to unify access codes across the whole organization, but management usually has things pretty compartmentalized. If you must, keep a notecard with your usernames and what programs they are for, but never write down passwords.

Invent a system for yourself, a code, pattern, or rubric, which you can use for all systems. Never use the same password for everything, but you can base a personal cryptography system on the websites or names of system folders themselves. It sounds more complicated than it is; all you do is take the name of the system you are accessing as a seed for a permutation, a long word that means variations on a set. In this case, the same variation every time. Alpha-numeric, alphabetical, and vowel drops are all common. Add the last name of an obscure friend, a place you love (any word you can easily recall but is pretty personal to you). Since numbers and special characters are often required, use L33t.

L33t uses numbers for letters, like the word l33t itself: the 3 looks a bit like an E. It is said "Leet," short for elite (although it has since gone mainstream); also typed out 1337. A little dated and certainly no longer the elite shorthand of coders but still helpful in making passwords. At the very least, use @ for "A," $ for "S," and ! for "I," and you should have the characters you need.

Test and Check

Test the cam, the mic, and any peripherals you might be using during the call. I find the sound is most likely to go squirrely (literally a high-pitched chipmunk error sometimes) but unplugging and plugging it back in usually helps. If the cam is part of the device, you can generally fix problems by closing and opening the camera or restarting your device.

If you are worried about it, make a test call to a friend or co-worker. Most professional settings are all too aware of the limitations of technology and will be forgiving of the occasional snafu. Snafu is actually descended from military jargon; when an organization gets so large, Situation Normal All F* Up means everyone will expect *something* to go wrong.

Tips for the Technologically Impaired
1. Close and reload the program.
2. Use Task Manager (ctrl+alt+del in Windows 10) if the program won't close normally.
3. Cycle the power; fancy IT talk for turn the thing off, wait 30 seconds, and turn it back on.
4. Reinstall; remove the program altogether (uninstall) and reinstall it; you will have to have IT do this for you in more secure networks.

5. Google the problem; the most challenging part of IT is often knowing technical terms and names for things.

Number five is critical because almost anything that can happen to you has happened to at least a hundred others, been cataloged, resolved, and posted with a troubleshooting guide online somewhere. Once you know technical terms for computer events and parts, what goes where, and how it all hooks together, you will have a marketable skill, if not a firmer handle on your workspace.

When you run into an error, freeze, or crash, go through the steps before contacting IT. I promise, if you need computer help or otherwise experience a technical difficulty, turning it on and off (the failing software first, then hardware it is running on) will solve the problem most of the time.

Stick to a single program package as much as possible or risk unprofessional interrupts, crashes, and even corruption. Microsoft, Google, and Apple offer extremely comprehensive business tools and comprehensive, interlocked systems that usually only require a single password.

BONUS - Take It Beyond the Inbox

As I mentioned before, the primary email format has remained unchanged since the Middle Ages. All our technology did was translate the written form into the digital. You can take many of the skills you've begun to develop before and apply them to projects outside of electronic mail. Not to fear, I'm not going to wrap up the guide trying to get you to learn calligraphy—no need when there's a program that imitates super-fine handwriting already. No, when we spread our wings and leave the comfortable nest of the normal inbox functions and take to the wild blue yonder that is web-based communication, the sky truly is the limit. Rich media, creative formats, and hyper-links give email the interactivity and allure you need to succeed.

When you can add not only sparkle (literal sparkle looks dated-don't use it) but one-clink interactivity, your email will not only speak for you but hold people's hands as it guides them exactly where you want them. With all these tools at your disposal, there is no reason not to make the most of your newfound skills. Recruiters and temp services hiring remote staff on websites and apps, all offering from full-time to gig work, the world has never been more open.

Typically used to supplement a primary income, as Covid forced the world to work remotely, many companies realized just how much of their workforce could be trans-located. The future seems to be online with less overhead and higher employee satisfaction.

Gig Work

What's your side hustle? Having a secondary revenue stream is never a bad idea; better yet, adding a third or more. Make sure you are leaving yourself free time, but this is a great way to get some quick cash. You're already online typing away; there is money to be made only a few clicks away. While finding a company to put you on the payroll is usually the best bet, it is even possible to make a living doing freelance remote work. If you intend to earn more than a secondary income, you will need quite a few sites and apps to pull from, the market is competitive, but there are so many job sites you can usually take your fill.

I recommend looking as broad as possible and investigating work that sounds *fun*. With the whole wide world to choose from, you will find a job, task, or project which intrigues you. Small-scale gig work is an excellent opportunity to try something out before you pursue it full time, as well as allow you to practice on something you ordinarily don't have a chance to. If stretching beyond your established skillset doesn't interest you, the interconnected world can offer you new possibilities within your chosen field, too.

Writing

If you're a wiz at English but never did anything with it, there is a whole wide world of content creators out there. If the creation of compelling email has hooked you, there are mass marketing companies specializing in creating professional emails. Not simply spam farms, these professional ad companies are usually called for "opt-in" or the emails you ask to receive.

There's far more to paid writing than emailed solicitations, of course. From ad copy to novels, paid reviews (all too common, I'm afraid), and running businesses' social media, you can very quickly take skills and abilities you develop working on electronic communication into many areas.

Podcasts, Videos, and Amateur Productions

You've done video conferences and are now comfortable in front of an audience, or at least comfortable faking it! In a world where virtual reality and high-definition images are becoming more and more common, it can seem like a surprise to learn that podcasts, basically internet radio shows, are on the rise. Video production equipment of extremely high quality is available to the average consumer. Even the cameras built into our smartphones are getting to the point where you can shoot entire movies from personal devices.

Podcasts

You may not want to put your smiling face out there, but if the written word is too dry for you, maybe think about doing a podcast. Make sure it is a topic you love, or at the very least will be able to go on at length about. No subject is too minute. In fact, many niche podcasts wind up getting popular *because* the topic is so obscure. The Lockpicking Lawyer comes to mind- I have no intention of picking locks, but the delivery is soothing and information oddly fascinating.

Record, review, and redo are essential with any production, so unless you want the undeniable spark that comes from a live broadcast, you rarely use the first take. You can snip out mistakes, record over errors, and otherwise correct minor flubs, so **if you have a post-production period, don't make your talent repeat themselves unless you have to**. This is where the sound engineer with headphones behind glass comes into play- actively listen for what can be corrected later versus what needs to be completely redone.

If you are the talent yourself, practice altering pace, change the tone, and mix up the delivery if you have time. Find an ideal combination for your voice and temperament; loosen up, have fun with it. Make fake commercials, parody newscasts, and anything to make you laugh so you can get comfortable and find your voice. Fair warning, if you play around with making recordings long enough, **your everyday speaking voice improves**, too. You can improve your tone of voice like any skill, so don't be shy with the redo's. Change pitch, try a little higher or a little lower; your production voice may be slightly different from your normal speaking voice but put too much flex on it, and it will come off sounding like a put on.

Post-production is always a good idea, and there are free audio editing suites (Audacity, for instance) that you can use to "sweeten" sounds. Editing is also how you would add sounds, either F/X or soundtrack. Make sure you remove any distracting flubs or mic noise at this stage, too.

Video

While not for everyone, video production's "cost of admission" has been dropping for decades. It is pretty easy for a layperson to get their hands on professional multimedia capture equipment, with libraries and maker spaces giving people an opportunity to play with the technology before deciding to purchase their own. Cable access studios still exist, and typically their only stipulation is a modest fee and a class before you can check out and use their real-deal pro stuff. I take that back- they will almost always ask you to make something they can put on the air.

Video software gets pricey, so take advantage of trial periods and demo packages before shelling out your hard-earned cash. Free and watermarked (company logo insert into every shot) software exists, though you may wind up moving a file from program to program because the more features a movie editing suite has, the more likely it is to be at cost.

As everything, record, review, and redo, and always be mindful of what can come out in editing; flubs, gaffs, and mistakes can be cut out, just like audio. You can use different programs to add titles and graphics of all kinds. In a professional setting, limit those to highlighting what the visual is and keep them contrasting to the background.

The Possibilities Are Endless

If I had told you ten years ago that internet rabble would be cable of storming the US capitol and shutting down a major Canadian city, you might think me crazy. Obama's campaign was undeniably the first to really lean into the internet age. The mob Trump was able to raise was so devoted they continue to deny the results of the 2020 election. The Information Age gives you what you want for better or worse. I joke, but the fact remains the internet and online communication has reached the point where you can begin weighing the good against the bad.

Use your feelings to find a perfect job for you, but that has to be weighed against your abilities and reasonable outcomes. Getting in touch with your emotions is crucial, but giving up executive decision-making to them leads to ruin. A little deep for a chapter on taking email etiquette to the next level, but it seems the US has lost its civility and ability to separate logic from emotion. Avoid getting into "flame-wars," online arguments with strangers which end up becoming consensus circle-jerks when believers on either side get attracted and begin agreeing with each other endlessly. A constructive conversation will always teach you something, even if you do not agree.

Take The Next Step

The saying I love the most, which motivated me to add book writing to my skill set, is "shoot for the moon because even if you miss, you'll wind up among the stars." In practical terms, all that means is if you want to be a doctor (for instance) but scrub out of medical school, chances are you now have credits toward a career in the medical field. Try writing a novel, write down those killer business model ideas, and otherwise dare to dream. Work, polish, and revise, but then share, submit, and try out!

Usually, you have nothing to lose but your time. The real test of a successful person is not learning how to win but learning how to fail. If you can be rejected repeatedly but believe in your product so much to rework and keep trying, you will find a foothold.

Dreams come true one step at a time, one win at a time (often after dozens or hundreds of losses), so never let an obstacle become a wall.

Conclusion

There are no postscripts in professional correspondence, but since I did format the top like a friendly letter, I thought I had better give you a proper, old-fashioned send-off.

There is so much hateful vitriol in the world. I beg you not to add to it. Sometimes a little heat is warranted, but always be sure to give the recipient a compliment sandwich (good-bad-good) or at least follow it up with constructive advice. If you can't say anything nice, don't say anything at all is OK up to a point, but if the person is headed toward disaster, you just might have to be the bearer of bad news. With a bit of consideration and empathy, you can deliver even unpleasant news in a way that will *at least* leave the recipient grateful for the information, if not happy to receive it.

Always remember that unsolicited advice *never* goes over as well as you'd like, and while it can be challenging to watch someone make a mistake unless you have trust or a truly gifted way with words, people need to be left to learn things on their own.

You don't have to be kind, but you do have to be civil. The golden rule applies, so if you were raised by wolves or just neglected basic social skills: you speak to others the way you would want to be spoken to. Make kind, precise, concise delivery your default setting, and at least email communication will never trouble you again.

More by Lawrence Finnegan

Discover all books from the Communication Skills Series by

Lawrence Finnegan at:

bit.ly/lawrence-finnegan

Book 1: Body Language

Book 2: Assertiveness

Book 3: Conversation Skills

Book 4: Persuasion

Book 5: Make People Laugh

Book 6: Small Talk

Book 7: Social Skills

Book 8: Email Etiquette

Themed book bundles available at discounted prices:

bit.ly/lawrence-finnegan